The Resilient Mind

The Resilient Mind

Matthew Petchinsky

1

The Resilient Mind: Thriving in Tough Times
By: Matthew Petchinsky

Disclaimer

The Resilient Mind: Thriving in Tough Times is a creative, educational, and motivational resource designed to support readers in developing inner strength, emotional clarity, and practical resilience skills. The strategies, insights, tools, and exercises presented throughout this book are intended for personal growth, self-reflection, and empowerment. They do **not** replace medical, psychiatric, psychological, legal, financial, or professional advice of any kind.

This book does **not** diagnose, treat, cure, or prevent any physical, mental, or emotional condition. If you are experiencing severe stress, anxiety, depression, trauma, or any condition that affects your safety or well-being, please consult a licensed healthcare professional, therapist, or qualified specialist. Never disregard professional guidance based on information contained within these pages.

All stories, examples, metaphors, frameworks, and concepts included in this book are for illustrative and educational purposes only. Any resemblance to real individuals, events, or situations is coincidental unless explicitly stated otherwise. The author makes no claims of guaranteed outcomes, specific results, or universal effectiveness. Personal results vary according to individual circumstances, choices, and levels of engagement.

Every exercise and recommendation within this book should be practiced mindfully, responsibly, and at your own pace. You are solely responsible for your decisions, actions, and interpretations. The author, publisher, and associated entities disclaim any liability for injury, loss, or consequences arising from the application of any content presented herein.

This book is free from religious doctrine or affiliation and does not reflect or promote the beliefs of any organized religion. It is written with the intent to support readers from all backgrounds while respecting diverse perspectives and experiences.

By reading this book, you acknowledge that the content is offered "as is" for educational enrichment and personal exploration. Your journey of resilience is unique, and the tools provided are meant to enhance—never replace—your own judgment, intuition, and professional support when needed.

Introduction: The Quiet Power That Changes Everything

Life will test you—sometimes slowly, sometimes all at once. You will face moments where plans collapse, people disappoint you, the world feels unpredictable, and your own energy seems to vanish without warning. These moments aren't signs of failure. They're invitations to rise.

Resilience is not about never breaking. It's about learning how to build yourself back in a stronger shape every time life tries to bend you.

It is the invisible foundation beneath every form of success—whether emotional, financial, physical, or spiritual. Resilience shapes how quickly you recover, how confidently you move forward, and how powerfully you navigate challenges that would destroy someone who never built internal strength.

Every successful person—whether a leader, creator, entrepreneur, athlete, survivor, or visionary—shares one quiet common denominator: **They keep going.** They experience setbacks, but they refuse to stay stuck in them. They get knocked down, but the ground never becomes their identity. Their resiliency becomes the force that redefines their future.

In a world where stress is constant, uncertainty is normal, and pressure is unavoidable, resilience is not optional—it is the single most valuable internal skill you can develop. Without resilience, motivation collapses, plans unravel, and opportunities slip away. But with resilience, you transform adversity into fuel, discomfort into growth, and obstacles into stepping-stones that push you toward your next breakthrough.

Why Resilience Is the Key to Success

Success is not linear. It is built inside the friction of effort, missteps, and constant recalibration. You don't succeed because everything goes right—you succeed because you learn how to keep moving when everything goes wrong.

Resilience is the key to success because:

1. Challenges Are Inevitable—But Defeat Doesn't Have to Be

Every goal, dream, or transformation comes with obstacles. Without resilience, these moments stop your progress. With resilience, they become catalysts for skill, wisdom, and maturity.

2. Resilient People Adapt Faster

Life changes without warning. Resilient individuals pivot, adjust, and respond without collapsing into frustration. Adaptability is the currency of long-term achievement.

3. Emotional Stability Fuels Consistent Action

Success requires sustained effort. Resilience protects your emotional well-being, keeps your mind focused, and strengthens your ability to show up—even on difficult days.

4. Confidence Grows From Survival, Not Ease

You don't feel confident because everything is comfortable. You feel confident because you've proven to yourself that you can survive what once felt impossible.

5. Resilience Elevates Decision-Making

A resilient mind thinks clearly under pressure. You make smarter choices, avoid impulsive reactions, and stay aligned with long-term goals instead of short-term relief.

Resilience is not just a skill—it is an identity.

A resilient person does not crumble.

A resilient mind does not retreat.
A resilient spirit transforms every challenge into a blueprint for elevation.

Steps to Bounce Back Stronger

You don't just "bounce back." You rebuild. You upgrade. You emerge different from who you were before the setback. Resilience is a process—a series of intentional steps that help you reclaim your power and rise with greater clarity.

Below are the core steps you will master throughout this book:

Step 1: Pause and Acknowledge What Happened

Resilience begins with honesty. You cannot rebuild what you refuse to recognize. Naming the challenge gives you power over it.

Step 2: Regulate Your Internal State

Emotional regulation restores your clarity.

Deep breathing, grounding practices, journaling, or brief stillness help you shift from chaos into stability, so you can approach the situation with strength instead of reactivity.

Step 3: Reframe the Meaning of the Setback

A setback is not a dead end—it is a redirection, a lesson, or a refinement of your path. Changing the narrative transforms defeat into opportunity.

Step 4: Identify What You Can Control

Resilient people don't waste energy on the uncontrollable. They focus on decisions, behaviors, and actions that shift their future.

Step 5: Create a Simple Recovery Plan

Small, manageable steps rebuild momentum. Progress doesn't require perfection—it requires movement.

Step 6: Strengthen Your Internal Environment

Your thoughts, habits, and self-talk either weaken or empower you. Resilience grows when you cultivate an inner environment where courage and clarity thrive.

Step 7: Move Forward With Renewed Purpose

Every bounce-back moment is an opportunity to reinvent yourself. You rise not as who you were—but as who you are becoming. That transformation is the heartbeat of resilience.

This book is your guide through that transformation.

It will teach you how to understand your mind, regulate your emotions, reinforce your identity, and rise into a stronger, sharper, more unshakable version of yourself.

You deserve a life where you thrive—not just survive.

Let this be the beginning of that rise.

Chapter 1: Understanding Resilience

Resilience is not an accident, a personality trait, or a gift that only a select few possess. It is a trained internal architecture—a framework of thoughts, habits, beliefs, and emotional patterns that determines how you navigate stress, uncertainty, and adversity. To understand resilience is to understand the subtle mechanics of your mind: how you interpret events, how you respond to challenges, how you process emotions, and how you build meaning out of your experiences.

Resilience doesn't eliminate hardship. It transforms the relationship you have with it.

People often imagine resilience as "being strong" or "never breaking," but true resilience is far more nuanced. It is not rigidity—it is flexibility. It is not emotional numbness—it is emotional intelligence. It is not blind positivity—it is grounded clarity. Resilience is the art of bending without collapsing, shifting without losing yourself, and recovering without losing momentum.

It is the quiet ability to say, "This is difficult, but I am not done."

When you cultivate resilience, you become someone who adapts rather than avoids, grows rather than retreats, and recalibrates rather than collapses. You become your own anchor—steady, centered, and rooted—even when the world around you feels unstable.

Understanding resilience begins with examining its core components: mindset, regulation, interpretation, and integration.

The Mindset Behind Resilience

The foundation of resilience begins in the mind. It is shaped by the internal narratives you repeat, the beliefs you hold about yourself, and the expectations you carry into each challenge.

A resilient mindset includes:

- **Growth Over Defeat**

Challenges are not endings—they are lessons wrapped in discomfort. Resilient people expect growth, not perfection.

- **Adaptive Thinking**

Instead of asking, "Why is this happening to me?" a resilient mind asks, "What can I do with this?"

- **Emotional Realism**

Resilience does not require pretending everything is fine. You can acknowledge difficulty while remaining anchored in possibility.

- **Internal Trust**

A resilient person may not know exactly how things will work out, but they trust their ability to figure it out.

The mindset behind resilience is not about being fearless—it is about moving forward **despite** fear.

Emotional Regulation: The Core Strength of Resilience

Resilience depends on how well you can navigate your internal world—not how well you hide it.

Stress, overwhelm, sadness, anger, and disappointment are natural human responses. But when emotions take over, thinking becomes reactive, actions become impulsive, and perspective becomes distorted. Emotional regulation is the process of grounding yourself before responding—so you act from clarity rather than chaos.

A regulated nervous system allows you to:

- Think before reacting
- Choose responses that align with your values
- Remain calm under pressure
- Notice opportunities hidden inside challenges
- Preserve energy rather than waste it on overwhelm

Emotional regulation is not suppression. It is mastery.

Interpretation: How You Explain Life to Yourself

Two people can experience the same event and walk away with entirely different stories. This is because experience is not defined by the event—it is defined by the meaning you assign to it.

Your interpretation shapes your resilience.

- **If you interpret setbacks as proof of inadequacy, resilience weakens.**
- **If you interpret setbacks as opportunities for refinement, resilience strengthens.**

Your mind is always telling a story. The question is:

Is it a story that diminishes you—or one that elevates you?

A resilient interpretation doesn't lie. It reframes.

It asks questions that lead to empowerment, not defeat.

Integration: Turning Hardship Into Inner Power

Understanding resilience means understanding that adversity holds information. Every challenge teaches you something about your limits, your strengths, your patterns, your wounds, and your potential.

Integration is the process of absorbing wisdom from difficulties rather than merely surviving them.

When you integrate hardship, you develop:

- Emotional maturity
- Mental clarity
- Inner confidence
- Spiritual grounding
- A deeper sense of identity
- A stronger commitment to your goals

Integration turns pain into purpose, wounds into wisdom, and setbacks into stepping-stones.

The Resilient Identity: Becoming the Person Who Rises

True resilience becomes part of your identity.

You move from trying to be resilient to **being** resilient.

A resilient identity is shaped by:

- Consistent recovery
- Consistent reflection
- Consistent self-awareness
- Consistent forward movement

Over time, resilience stops being something you practice and becomes something you embody. You become the person who rises—not because life is easy, but because you refuse to stay down.

Understanding resilience is the first step toward mastering it. Every chapter that follows will help you build deeper layers of strength, clarity, and emotional fortitude.

Journal Prompts – Chapter 1: Understanding Resilience
Use these prompts to access deeper clarity and self-awareness.

1. When was the last time I surprised myself with my resilience? What did I learn from that experience?
2. What beliefs do I currently hold about my ability to handle stress or adversity?
3. How do I typically respond in the first 10 minutes of a challenge or setback?
4. Which emotions are the hardest for me to regulate, and why?
5. What internal story do I tell myself when something goes wrong?
6. How has adversity in my past contributed to my strength today?
7. What patterns weaken my resilience, and which ones strengthen it?
8. What would a more resilient version of me do differently in daily life?
9. What does "bouncing back stronger" look like for me personally?
10. If I trusted myself 50% more, how would my responses to challenges change?

Closing Reflection

Resilience begins with awareness—awareness of your thoughts, your emotional patterns, your narrative, and your identity. You have already endured storms that were meant to break you, yet you are here, reading, learning, and rising. This alone is proof that resilience is not something you lack; it is something you have always carried.

As you move forward in this book, let this truth anchor you:

You are capable of becoming stronger than your circumstances.
Not because hardship disappears, but because you are learning how to stand taller in the midst of it.

Carry this wisdom with you as you step into the next chapter: Resilience is not a destination—it is a way of being. And you are building it, moment by moment, from the inside out.

Chapter 2: Managing Emotional Stress

Emotional stress doesn't simply appear—it accumulates. It gathers inside your mind, your breath, your muscles, and your daily reactions until you eventually feel weighed down by pressure that never had a proper outlet. Stress is the body's way of signaling imbalance, overload, or a need for change. But emotional stress becomes manageable when you understand how to regulate it, release it, and transform it into clarity rather than chaos.

Managing emotional stress begins with learning how to stabilize your internal environment. When you can steady yourself internally, external stress loses its ability to control your reactions. This chapter explores practical emotional-regulation tools, grounding strategies, natural supports like calming stones, restorative teas, and meditative practices designed to help you regain your center.

Emotional stress is not a flaw—it's a message. It's a signal that something needs attention, support, or recalibration. Your job is not to suppress the signal but to respond to it with intelligence, compassion, and structure. With the right tools, emotional stress becomes an opportunity to strengthen your inner stability.

Each of the following six sections will guide you deeper into the art of emotional management, helping you anchor your nervous system, regulate your thoughts, and reclaim your personal power.

Understanding the Physiology of Emotional Stress

Emotional stress is not "in your head"—it is a full-body experience. When your brain perceives pressure or uncertainty, it activates the sympathetic nervous system, releasing cortisol and adrenaline. These chemicals are useful during danger but draining during daily life. That is why emotional stress can feel physically exhausting even when nothing "big" has happened.

Your breathing shifts when stress rises. It becomes shallow, uneven, or rapid. This disrupts oxygen flow, increases tension, and makes even small challenges feel overwhelming. Understanding this physiological response allows you to interrupt the cycle. When you change your breathing, you change your brain chemistry—helping you reset your emotional state.

Stress also affects your muscles. The shoulders tighten. The jaw locks. The stomach clenches. These tension patterns become habitual and silently drain your energy. When you learn to release these physical signatures of stress, your emotional load lightens as well. The body and the mind mirror each other.

By understanding stress as a chemistry, not a character flaw, you gain control. Stress becomes something you influence rather than something that dominates your day. Awareness is the first step toward mastery.

Calming Your Nervous System Through Breath and Rhythm

Breathwork is one of the fastest ways to regulate your emotional state because it speaks directly to the nervous system. Slow, deep breathing activates the parasympathetic system—your internal "calm switch." It lowers cortisol, stabilizes your heart rate, and clears mental fog within minutes.

A simple technique is **4-6 breathing**: inhale for four seconds, exhale for six. The extended exhale signals to the body that it is safe. Practicing this for even one minute can interrupt spiraling thoughts and reduce tension. This is especially powerful during overwhelm, arguments, or moments when your emotions feel louder than your logic.

Rhythmic movement also regulates stress. Gentle walking, stretching, rocking motions, or shoulder rolls help release the energy trapped inside your muscles. Movement turns emotional pressure into momentum rather than stagnation. The body processes what the mind cannot yet articulate.

When you pair breath with movement—slow walking, stretching, or pacing intentionally—you create a powerful internal harmony. This becomes your emotional reset button, letting you shift from reactive to grounded in minutes.

Twelve Stones for Managing Emotional Stress

Certain stones are traditionally used to stabilize emotions, regulate energy, and calm the nervous system. Whether used as pocket stones, placed under pillows, or held during meditation, each one carries unique balancing qualities.

• **Amethyst**

Calms mental clutter and reduces overthinking. Known for promoting peace and aiding sleep during stressful periods. Helps release emotional agitation.

• **Rose Quartz**

Softens emotional wounds, encourages self-compassion, and relieves feelings of emotional tightness or sadness. Supports heart-centered healing.

• **Black Tourmaline**

Anchors the mind during stress. Deflects chaotic emotional energy and helps you stay grounded when your thoughts feel scattered or heavy.

• **Lepidolite**

Rich in natural lithium. Known for easing anxiety, stabilizing mood fluctuations, and helping the mind shift out of panic into clarity.

• **Selenite**

Cleanses emotional residue and creates mental spaciousness. Helpful for decompressing after heavy conversations or long days.

• **Blue Lace Agate**

Gentle stone for emotional communication. Helps calm panic, soothe emotional overwhelm, and restore calmness to the throat and chest.

• **Smoky Quartz**

Absorbs stress, fear, and worry. Excellent for people who feel overstimulated, pressured, or weighed down.

• **Howlite**

Slows an overactive mind. Encourages patience, emotional pacing, and clarity during high-pressure situations.

• **Labradorite**

Protects emotional boundaries and reduces energy drains from conflict, negativity, or emotional tension in the environment.

• **Moonstone**

Balances internal fluctuations, soothes emotional waves, and supports emotional recalibration during stressful transitions or uncertainty.

• **Hematite**

Grounds and stabilizes the mind. Helpful for returning to logic when stress has created reactive thinking.

• **Green Aventurine**

Restores optimism, emotional freshness, and inner peace. Helps reset the mood after disappointment or frustration.

These stones are not magical fixes—they are tools that support your emotional regulation practices. Their stability encourages your stability.

Four Calming Tea Recipes + Deep Meditative Practices

Tea rituals help calm stress by combining warmth, breath, aroma, and mindfulness. These four teas include optional meditations designed to enhance emotional grounding.

Tea 1: Chamomile–Lavender Harmony Tea

Ingredients:

- 1 tbsp dried chamomile
- 1 tsp dried lavender
- 1 tsp honey
- Hot water

Meditation:

Hold the warm cup between your palms. Inhale the floral scent, imagining it softening mental tension. On each exhale, release one worry. Continue until the tea cools. Let the heat melt stress trapped in your chest.

Tea 2: Ginger–Lemon Stability Tea
Ingredients:

- 4 thin slices fresh ginger
- Juice of ½ lemon
- 1 tsp maple syrup
- Hot water

Meditation:

As you sip, imagine the ginger igniting strength inside you while the lemon clears emotional fog. Breathe deeply with each sip. Visualize stress dissolving into warmth that spreads through your whole body.

Tea 3: Peppermint–Honey Clarity Tea
Ingredients:

- 1 tbsp dried peppermint
- 1 tsp honey
- Hot water

Meditation:
Place your hand on your stomach. Breathe deeply and feel the cool scent clearing your mind. With each sip, imagine mental clutter drifting away like mist. Let coolness bring emotional neutrality.

Tea 4: Rooibos–Vanilla Comfort Tea
Ingredients:

- 1 tbsp rooibos tea
- 2–3 drops pure vanilla extract
- Optional: 1 cinnamon stick
- Hot water

Meditation:
Sit in silence as you drink. Visualize a protective warmth surrounding you, like a soft glow. With every sip, repeat internally: *"I am safe. I am grounded. I am centered."*

Reframing Emotional Stress Into Emotional Data

Emotional stress becomes overwhelming when it is misunderstood. But when you view stress as information instead of an enemy, everything changes. Stress tells you something about your boundaries, your responsibilities, your energy levels, and your needs.

When stress rises, ask:

"What is this emotion trying to tell me?"

Stress may be signaling exhaustion. Or unmet needs. Or emotional pressure. Or a situation that requires change. The moment you begin interpreting stress, you stop drowning in it.

Reframing stress is not about denying your feelings. It is about decoding them. It transforms emotional heaviness into wisdom. It shifts you from victim to observer, from overwhelmed to informed.

Through reframing, stress becomes guidance. That single shift helps you move from being controlled by your emotions to using them as data for growth.

Building a Stress-Resilient Identity

Managing emotional stress ultimately becomes part of who you are. When you consistently regulate your emotions, support your nervous system, and interpret stress with clarity, you begin to develop an identity that does not collapse under pressure.

A stress-resilient identity is built through micro-practices: small moments of choosing calm over chaos, grounding over reactivity, and understanding over panic. These moments accumulate, strengthening your emotional backbone.

Over time, you begin trusting yourself more. Stress no longer feels like a threat, because you've proven—repeatedly—that you can regulate it. You can stabilize yourself. You can choose your response.

When managing emotional stress becomes part of your identity, you enter a new chapter of personal power. Stress may still appear—but it no longer defines you.

Journal Prompts – Chapter 2: Managing Emotional Stress

1. What physical sensations do I notice first when emotional stress begins?
2. Which breathing practices help me feel grounded most effectively?
3. What triggers consistently elevate my stress levels?
4. How do I typically react when emotions escalate quickly?
5. Which stone from the list resonates with me most, and why?
6. What boundaries do I need to enforce to reduce stress?
7. What thoughts usually worsen my stress, and which thoughts help reduce it?
8. When was the last time I handled stress in a healthy, empowered way?
9. What does my ideal "calm self" look and feel like?
10. What stress patterns am I ready to break starting today?

Closing Reflection

Stress does not define you—it reveals you. It shows you where healing is needed, where boundaries are thin, where rest is overdue, and where your growth is asking for attention. Every time you manage emotional stress with awareness, breath, grounding, and choice, you strengthen the architecture of your resilience.

You are not meant to be overwhelmed forever. You are meant to learn your own inner wiring so well that stress becomes something you meet with confidence, not fear. Carry this truth forward:

You are capable of managing emotional storms with clarity, strength, and calmness.

Your resilience grows every time you choose understanding over reaction.

Chapter 3: Rebuilding After a Setback

Setbacks are not signs of failure—they are interruptions that force you to pause, reassess, and rise in a stronger form. Every setback, whether personal, financial, emotional, or physical, creates a fracture in your path. But fractures are not the end. They are openings for redesign, opportunities for refinement, and invitations to evolve.

Rebuilding after a setback requires honesty, courage, and a willingness to face the reality of what happened without letting it define you. Many people get stuck in the emotional debris of a setback, replaying the moment endlessly or blaming themselves for what cannot be undone. But true resilience comes from recognizing that the past is information—not identity. What happened informs your next move, but it does not determine who you are becoming.

Rebuilding is not just about recovery—it is about **reconstruction**. You are not returning to who you were before the setback. You are constructing a more informed, stronger, and more self-aware version of yourself. Setbacks reveal your weak points, but they also reveal your potential. They show you what needs strengthening, what needs releasing, and what deserves a new structure altogether.

This chapter will guide you through the essential stages of rebuilding: acknowledging, processing, learning, re-structuring, and rising with intention. Each stage is a form of liberation. Every step you take is a declaration that you are not defined by what broke—you are defined by how you rebuild.

The Importance of Honest Acknowledgment

A setback cannot be healed if it cannot be named. Many people rush past the acknowledgment stage, either out of discomfort or out of fear that facing the truth will confirm their worst worries. But denial traps you; honesty frees you.

Acknowledgment is about describing what happened without judgment. It's not about guilt, shame, or self-blame. It is about clarity. When you see the situation clearly, you can see your next steps clearly too. Clarity is the foundation of rebuilding.

When you avoid acknowledging a setback, you carry its weight silently. The unspoken becomes emotional baggage, mental pressure, and internal heaviness. But when you acknowledge it—when you say, "Yes, this happened, and it affected me"—you release the emotional tension that was keeping you stuck.

Honesty is not weakness. It's the first step toward your comeback story. You cannot rebuild a structure you refuse to examine. Acknowledgment gives you the blueprint for reconstruction.

Processing the Emotional Impact

Every setback has an emotional aftershock. Whether the setback was sudden or predictable, your body and mind react. You may feel embarrassment, fear, sadness, frustration, or confusion. All of these emotions are valid. They are your mind's way of signaling that something meaningful occurred.

Processing these emotions requires patience and self-compassion. Rushing yourself through emotional recovery only creates more emotional residue. Healing takes time. It takes breathing room, gentleness, and space to feel without drowning in the feeling.

When you process emotions instead of suppressing them, you prevent them from becoming long-term emotional patterns that affect your identity. Unprocessed emotions become self-doubt, avoidance, anxiety, or defensiveness. But processed emotions become wisdom.

Emotion is the language of your inner world. Processing it is how you translate your experiences into deeper awareness. Without emotional processing, rebuilding becomes fragile. With it, your foundation becomes unshakable.

Extracting Wisdom and Lessons From the Setback

Every setback carries information. Something didn't work, something was misaligned, or something needed to be confronted. Extracting the lessons from the setback is how you prevent history from repeating itself.

Reflection is not about obsessing over the past—it is about understanding it. It is about answering questions like:

- What contributed to the setback?
- What signs did I overlook?
- What strengths helped me endure it?
- What patterns do I need to change?

These questions turn pain into guidance.

Without extracting lessons, a setback feels meaningless. With lessons, a setback becomes meaningful growth. It becomes an upgrade, not a punishment. The moment you realize you can use the setback instead of suffering under it, you reclaim your power.

Wisdom gained through adversity becomes a lifelong resource. It becomes intuition, discernment, and foresight. It becomes the internal compass that helps you avoid future obstacles and navigate new challenges with confidence.

Rebuilding Your Inner Structure

Once the emotional dust settles and the lessons become clear, rebuilding begins. This is where resilience becomes action.

Rebuilding your inner structure means redesigning your thoughts, beliefs, habits, and boundaries in a way that supports your next evolution. It means removing what weakens you, reinforcing what strengthens you, and creating new frameworks that match your future—not your past.

This may involve:

- Strengthening your daily routines
- Establishing healthier boundaries
- Changing limiting beliefs
- Upgrading your environment
- Reinforcing supportive relationships
- Recommitting to your values

Rebuilding is both strategic and emotional. It requires discipline, but it also requires gentleness. It asks you to choose yourself daily. It transforms the setback from something that happened to you into something that shaped you.

When you rebuild, you don't merely bounce back—you rise above where you were before.

Regaining Momentum

Momentum is the bridge between recovery and transformation. After a setback, your energy can feel slow, heavy, or uncertain. That is normal. The key is to restart gently. You don't need massive action—you need consistent action.

Small steps matter. A 10-minute task, one page of writing, one conversation, one decision—each small movement creates traction. And traction creates confidence. Confidence creates momentum.

Think of momentum as a slow flame you gradually nurture. If you push too hard too quickly, you extinguish it. But if you nurture it steadily, it becomes a wildfire of progress.

Momentum grows through repetition, intention, and self-trust. Every step forward, no matter how small, rewires your identity:

"I am capable of rebuilding."

"I am moving forward."

"I am in control again."

These reinforcing identities fuel your comeback.

Rising Into Your Next Level

Rebuilding leads to rising. Your setback becomes the foundation of a stronger, more evolved version of yourself. Rising into your next level means stepping into the wisdom, clarity, and strength that the setback revealed.

This is where transformation happens. The version of you that rises after a setback is wiser, more grounded, more intentional, and more aware of your inner power. You gain confidence from having survived something difficult. You gain insight from having reflected on it. You gain resilience from having rebuilt after it.

Rising is not a sudden moment—it is a gradual unfolding. It is the moment you realize you are no longer defined by what happened. You are defined by who you became because of it.

Every setback contains a rise within it. And every rise opens the door to a new identity—one that moves through life with strength, purpose, and emotional intelligence.

Journal Prompts – Chapter 3: Rebuilding After a Setback

1. What setback has affected me the most recently, and how did it impact my emotions?
2. What part of the setback was outside my control, and what part was within my control?
3. What signs or patterns did I overlook before the setback happened?
4. What strengths helped me endure the experience?
5. What lessons am I meant to learn from this setback?
6. What beliefs about myself shifted because of this experience—positively or negatively?
7. What support, boundaries, or habits do I need to reinforce during my rebuilding process?
8. What small step can I take today to regain momentum?
9. How can I rebuild in a way that makes me stronger than before the setback?
10. Who am I becoming because of what I survived?

Closing Reflection

Rebuilding after a setback is one of the most courageous things a person can do. It requires facing truth, processing emotions, learning from difficulty, restructuring your inner world, and stepping forward even when the path is unclear. Every step you take is evidence of your resilience. Every moment of honesty, reflection, and forward movement shapes a stronger version of you.

You are not the same person you were before the setback—and that is a gift. You are wiser. You are deeper. You are more compassionate toward yourself. You are more aware of your strength. Your comeback is not defined by speed—it is defined by intention.

Walk forward knowing this:
Your setback was not the end. It was your beginning.
You are rebuilding something extraordinary—yourself.

Chapter 4: Developing Mental Toughness

Mental toughness is not about being emotionless, unbreakable, or hardened by life. True mental toughness is the ability to stay focused, grounded, and strategic even when the world around you feels uncertain, overwhelming, or chaotic. It is the skill that allows you to press forward when motivation fades, stay committed when emotions fluctuate, and remain confident even when doubt tries to creep in.

Mental toughness is the architecture of long-term resilience. It is the internal structure that supports your thoughts, stabilizes your reactions, and strengthens your identity. While resilience focuses on recovery, mental toughness focuses on endurance. Resilience helps you rise after you fall—mental toughness helps you keep walking forward without collapsing again.

In this chapter, you will explore the pillars of mental toughness: discipline, mindset control, emotional neutrality, identity strength, and long-term focus. These pillars work together to help you navigate pressure and maintain equilibrium even during difficult moments. You will learn to build an internal system that doesn't crumble at the first sign of struggle but instead becomes stronger under challenge.

Mental toughness is not something you are born with. It is cultivated through habits, refined through experience, and strengthened through conscious choices. With time and practice, it becomes your default operating system—your psychological armor.

The Foundation: Training Your Inner Dialogue

Every ounce of mental toughness begins with the conversations you have with yourself. Your inner dialogue shapes your self-perception, influences your behaviors, and determines your endurance under pressure. When your inner voice becomes a coach rather than a critic, mental toughness emerges naturally.

A weak inner dialogue collapses under stress. It focuses on fear, doubt, and potential failure. It magnifies obstacles and minimizes your abilities. But a disciplined inner dialogue reinforces truth, clarity, and capability. It fuels momentum rather than drains it.

Training your inner dialogue means learning to question thoughts that weaken you and amplify thoughts that strengthen you. It means replacing defeat-based self-talk with neutral or growth-based alternatives. It means noticing when you are catastrophizing and redirecting the narrative before emotional spiraling begins.

Mental toughness grows when you master your internal voice—not when you silence your emotions. Your inner dialogue becomes your internal coach, pushing you toward strength rather than surrender.

The Power of Emotional Neutrality

Mental toughness requires a specific emotional skill: **neutrality**. Emotional neutrality is the ability to experience your feelings without becoming controlled by them. It does not mean suppressing your emotions or pretending you are unaffected. Instead, it means observing emotions without letting them dictate your choices.

When you respond from emotional neutrality, you slow the reaction gap. Instead of reacting impulsively, you pause, breathe, and assess. You allow the emotion to move through you without letting it hijack your behavior. This is one of the most powerful tools for mental toughness because it preserves your decision-making ability under pressure.

Emotional neutrality strengthens mental toughness by creating distance between the stimulus and the reaction. It helps you avoid unnecessary conflict, reduce overthinking, and prevent emotional exhaustion. It allows clarity to replace chaos.

Becoming emotionally neutral does not make you less human. It makes you more effective. You learn to carry emotions without collapsing under them. You become the calm center in your life—even when everything around you feels turbulent.

Discipline: The Backbone of Mental Toughness

Discipline is where mental toughness becomes visible. It is the bridge between intention and action, desire and achievement, resilience and transformation. Discipline teaches your mind that your commitments matter more than your comfort.

A mentally tough person does not rely on motivation. They rely on structure. They rely on routines, boundaries, and consistent action—especially when they don't feel like it.

Discipline involves:

- Keeping promises to yourself
- Showing up even when energy fluctuates
- Following through on plans
- Prioritizing long-term growth over short-term relief
- Creating order where your emotions want chaos

When you develop discipline, you strengthen your internal authority. You stop negotiating with self-doubt. You stop collapsing under pressure. You build a mental identity that says, "I can depend on myself."

Discipline is not about perfection—it is about consistency. It is about proving to yourself that your actions can carry you through difficulty even when your emotions cannot.

Strengthening Your Identity

Mental toughness is inseparable from identity. You cannot act stronger than the identity you hold. If you see yourself as fragile, you will collapse. If you see yourself as capable, you will rise. Identity determines behavior.

To strengthen your identity, you must adopt internal beliefs that reinforce mental strength. These identity beliefs might include:

- "I can handle discomfort."
- "Pressure sharpens me."
- "I stay grounded when challenged."
- "I adapt quickly."
- "I remain calm under uncertainty."

Identity is not built through words alone—it is built through evidence. Each time you endure difficulty, regulate your emotions, or stay committed to your path, you reinforce a stronger identity. Over time, your mind begins to believe:
"I am someone who does not break."

Mental toughness becomes self-perpetuating when it becomes part of your identity. You no longer have to force it—it becomes who you are.

Expanding Your Tolerance for Discomfort

Mental toughness requires learning to coexist with discomfort rather than escape from it. Discomfort is where growth happens. It is the environment where strength is built, habits are reshaped, emotional endurance is formed, and self-control is refined.

Many people collapse under discomfort because they misinterpret it. They believe discomfort means danger or failure. But discomfort is simply the feeling of expansion. It is your system adjusting to a new level of challenge.

When you train your tolerance for discomfort, you learn to stay grounded during:

- Stress
- Uncertainty
- Fatigue
- Emotional friction
- Slow progress
- Difficult decisions

The goal is not to eliminate discomfort—it is to develop the capacity to function powerfully in its presence. Mental toughness grows every time you choose discipline over avoidance, presence over retreat, and progress over fear.

Long-Term Focus in a Short-Term World

Mental toughness thrives when you shift your focus from immediate reactions to long-term outcomes. Most emotional turbulence comes from short-term thinking—fear of temporary discomfort, frustration about slow results, or fixation on instant gratification.

Long-term focus changes your entire internal landscape. Suddenly:

- setbacks become temporary
- discomfort becomes a tool
- discipline becomes easier
- doubt becomes quieter
- consistency becomes meaningful

A long-term perspective builds patience, clarity, and emotional steadiness. You start valuing progress over speed, depth over distraction, and lasting transformation over momentary relief.

Mental toughness develops when you stop letting temporary emotions dictate lifelong decisions. When your goals become bigger than your discomfort, your mind becomes unstoppable.

Journal Prompts – Chapter 4: Developing Mental Toughness

1. What situations challenge my mental toughness the most, and why?
2. What negative inner dialogue patterns weaken me during stress?
3. How can I shift my self-talk from critical to supportive?
4. Which emotions tend to take control of my decisions?
5. What areas of my life need more discipline and structure?
6. How have I underestimated my own strength in the past?
7. What new identity beliefs can strengthen my mental resilience?
8. How do I currently respond to discomfort, and what response would be healthier?
9. What long-term goals matter enough to strengthen my mental toughness for?
10. What small daily habit would dramatically improve my mental strength over time?

Closing Reflection

Mental toughness is not about becoming hardened—it is about becoming unshakably clear, grounded, and self-led. It is the internal power that allows you to hold your center no matter what pressure surrounds you. Every step you take to strengthen your inner dialogue, practice emotional neutrality, expand your tolerance for discomfort, and commit to your long-term vision builds a version of you that life cannot easily break.

You are capable of extraordinary endurance. You are capable of consistency even when motivation fades. You are capable of holding your power even when emotions fluctuate. Mental toughness is not a performance—it is a quiet, disciplined, steady strength that grows inside you over time.

Carry this truth forward:

You are not at the mercy of your mind—you are the architect of it.

And the structure you build will support you for a lifetime.

Chapter 5: Turning Challenges Into Opportunities

Challenges are not interruptions—they are initiations. Every obstacle you face carries within it a coded opportunity, a hidden doorway, or a new direction waiting to be discovered. Most people spend their lives resisting challenges, fearing them, or wishing they would disappear. But resilient individuals understand something powerful: **challenges do not block your path—challenges *are* the path.**

Turning challenges into opportunities requires a shift in mindset. Instead of viewing difficulty as a threat, you begin to view it as raw material. Just as pressure turns carbon into diamonds, challenges shape your mindset, sharpen your decisions, and strengthen your identity. They force you to evolve beyond your comfort zone, expand your mental capacity, and grow into versions of yourself you didn't know existed.

Opportunities rarely arrive disguised as comfort. They arrive disguised as uncertainty, discomfort, pressure, or transition. When you know how to decode the challenges you face, you discover that every problem contains a possibility—and every possibility contains a future you haven't accessed yet.

This chapter will teach you how to transform challenges into catalysts, use adversity as a lever for growth, and rise into your next level with purpose and clarity.

The Perspective Shift: Seeing Challenges Through a New Lens

The first step in turning challenges into opportunities is rewriting the narrative you attach to difficulty. Most people meet challenges with fear-based interpretations: "This is too hard," "This shouldn't be happening," or "This means something is wrong." These interpretations create mental blocks that make progress harder.

But when you view challenges as teachers rather than threats, everything changes. You begin to ask empowering questions:

- *What is this challenge trying to show me?*
- *What skill is this moment forcing me to develop?*
- *How can this obstacle strengthen my resilience?*
- *What new path is being revealed?*

Perspective determines possibility. When your perspective shifts toward growth, challenges transform into stepping-stones, not roadblocks. You begin to see where resilience, strategy, creativity, or courage is needed. Challenges become assignments that prepare you for larger breakthroughs.

The world does not become easier—you become stronger.

Identifying Hidden Opportunities in Difficult Moments

Every challenge contains a hidden opportunity, but you must learn how to notice it. Challenges reveal weaknesses, push you into new environments, or highlight areas of your life that require reinforcement. These insights are invitations—opportunities in disguise.

A challenge may be an opportunity to:

- Strengthen emotional boundaries
- Build new skill sets
- Change outdated habits
- Reinvent your approach
- Expand your creativity
- Let go of something misaligned
- Step into a higher version of yourself

Sometimes the opportunity is obvious. Other times it appears slowly, revealing itself only after reflection. But it is always there.

When you ask, *"What opportunity is hiding in this challenge?"* your brain begins to search for solutions rather than staying trapped in overwhelm. Solutions appear when your mind is open to them. Opportunities reveal themselves when you are willing to look beyond the problem.

Building Strength Through Adversity

Adversity develops a kind of strength that comfort cannot. Easy times build ease—but hard times build character, resilience, inner stability, and emotional intelligence. You learn more about yourself during difficulty than during simplicity.

Strength built through adversity includes:

- The ability to endure uncertainty
- The capacity to think clearly under pressure
- Emotional grounding in chaos
- Trust in yourself during difficult decisions
- The courage to move forward without guarantees

Each time you navigate adversity, you reinforce your mental architecture. You prove to yourself that you can persevere. You expand your belief in your ability to survive discomfort, conflict, or change.

This strength becomes transferable. Once you learn how to handle one challenge with confidence, you carry that skill into every new experience. Adversity becomes training—not punishment.

Unlocking Creativity Through Constraint

Challenges force creativity. When resources, time, energy, or options become limited, your brain becomes sharper. Constraint requires innovation. It pushes you to think differently, see differently, and act differently.

Creativity activated by challenge is one of the most valuable forms of problem-solving because it emerges from necessity, not convenience. It encourages:

- New strategies
- New perspectives
- New solutions
- New levels of efficiency
- New levels of adaptability

Some of the greatest breakthroughs, inventions, and personal transformations in human history happened because people were pushed to their limits. Challenge cracks open dimensions of creativity that comfort cannot access.

When you meet a challenge and ask,

"How can I use what I have in a new way?"

your mind enters a higher state of innovation. That state is where opportunity lives.

Rising With Purpose

This is the moment where challenge transforms into meaning, and struggle transforms into direction. Rising with purpose means using the momentum of adversity to propel you into a deeper mission, a clearer path, or a more grounded identity.

Purpose is born from friction. It emerges when you decide that your setbacks will not be wasted. It grows when you find meaning in what was meant to break you and turn that meaning into fuel.

Rising with purpose involves:

- Recognizing how your challenges shape who you are becoming
- Seeing your personal struggles as stepping-stones toward your mission
- Allowing adversity to refine—not define—you
- Choosing intention over reactivity
- Letting your resilience guide your next chapter

Purpose transforms challenge into alignment. It repurposes pain into clarity. It teaches you that every difficulty shaped your character in ways that ease never could. Purpose gives your journey direction and gives your efforts meaning.

When you rise with purpose, your challenges become part of your strength story—not your struggle story.

Turning Action Into Transformation

Identifying the opportunity in a challenge is only the beginning. True transformation requires action. It requires choosing one step, one new habit, one new mindset, or one new direction that moves you forward.

Action does not need to be dramatic. Small, consistent movement creates large-scale transformation. One shift in behavior creates ripples across your entire path. The key is committing to movement—even if the movement is slow.

Transformation occurs when:

- You apply the lessons
- You reinforce the growth
- You take consistent steps
- You choose courage, not retreat
- You align your actions with your purpose

Challenges can be catalysts—but only if you use them. When you take action, you transform potential into progress and progress into elevation.

You do not rise by wishing for better circumstances.
You rise by using the circumstances you have to build something better.

Journal Prompts – Chapter 5: Turning Challenges Into Opportunities

1. What challenge am I currently facing, and what opportunity might be hidden within it?
2. How have past challenges shaped my resilience or identity?
3. What strengths have I gained specifically from adversity?
4. What new perspective can I adopt to see this challenge differently?
5. What limiting beliefs surface when I experience difficulty?
6. How can this challenge encourage me to grow or evolve?
7. What creative solutions can emerge from the constraints I'm facing?
8. What purpose might be rising from this struggle?
9. What is one action I can take today to transform this challenge into progress?
10. Who am I becoming because I am choosing to rise through this?

Closing Reflection

Challenges will visit your life again and again—not to defeat you, but to elevate you. Each one carries a lesson, a doorway, or a breakthrough waiting to awaken. When you choose to view challenges as opportunities, you shift from survival mode to transformation mode. You begin to rise with intention, respond with clarity, and grow with purpose.

You are not shaped by what happens—you are shaped by how you use what happens.

Let every challenge sharpen you. Let every obstacle refine you. Let every setback redirect you toward a stronger version of yourself. You are powerful not because your path is easy, but because you continue to rise—again and again—with purpose guiding your steps.

Your challenges do not diminish you.
They unveil you.

Appendix A: 100 Journal Prompts for Transforming Resilience

Use these prompts to deepen your self-awareness, strengthen emotional clarity, expand your resilience, and evolve into your strongest self. Write without judgment. Let your thoughts flow freely.

SECTION 1 — Understanding Yourself

1. What emotions do I feel most often, and what triggers them?
2. What belief about myself has held me back the most?
3. Where do I feel the most confident in my life? Why?
4. What makes me feel mentally strong?
5. What patterns repeat in my life, and what might they be teaching me?
6. Which areas of my life feel aligned, and which feel misaligned?
7. When do I feel like my "truest self"?
8. What strengths have I underestimated in myself?
9. What fears influence my behavior the most?
10. How do I define resilience in my own words?
11. What does emotional stability look like to me?
12. What situations make me feel the most grounded?
13. What is one limiting belief I'm ready to challenge?
14. What decision from my past made me proud of myself?
15. How have past hardships shaped my identity?
16. What qualities do I admire in mentally strong individuals?
17. What makes me feel overwhelmed, and why?
18. What internal stories do I repeat that need updating?
19. When do I feel most disconnected from myself?
20. What parts of myself am I ready to rediscover?

SECTION 2 — Navigating Emotions

1. What emotions are hardest for me to process?
2. How do I usually respond when my emotions intensify?
3. What physical signs tell me I'm stressed?
4. What emotion do I tend to avoid?
5. How do I soothe myself in healthy ways?
6. What unhealthy coping habits do I want to let go of?
7. What emotion do I need to give myself permission to feel today?
8. How can I show myself compassion during emotional struggles?
9. What triggers my anxiety, and why?
10. What does emotional safety mean to me?
11. How do I react when I feel misunderstood?
12. What past emotional wound still affects me today?
13. How do I calm my body when it enters stress mode?
14. What inner dialogue appears during emotional chaos?
15. How can I shift my self-talk during difficult moments?
16. What perspective do I gain after emotional storms pass?
17. What emotion teaches me the most about myself?
18. When did I last feel emotionally strong?
19. What does emotional honesty feel like to me?
20. How can I create more emotional space for myself?

SECTION 3 — Rebuilding After Setbacks

1. What recent setback impacted me the most?
2. What part of the setback was beyond my control?
3. What part of it can I learn from?
4. How did I rise the last time life knocked me down?
5. What strengths helped me survive a difficult time?
6. What did a past setback teach me about resilience?
7. What could I do differently next time?
8. What boundaries need strengthening after the setback?
9. How did the setback shift my identity?
10. What new values emerged from that experience?
11. What habits contributed to the setback?
12. What habits can prevent future setbacks?
13. What does rebuilding look like for me right now?
14. Where am I still holding emotional residue from a setback?
15. What would full healing look like?
16. What small step will help me rebuild momentum?
17. What strengths do I want to carry forward?
18. What old version of myself am I outgrowing?
19. How do I celebrate progress when rebuilding?
20. What does a powerful comeback look like to me?

SECTION 4 — Developing Mental Toughness

1. What challenges strengthen me the most?
2. What distractions weaken my mental focus?
3. What qualities make someone mentally tough?
4. What identity beliefs increase my resilience?
5. How do I show up on days I don't feel motivated?
6. What routines make me feel mentally stable?
7. What inner dialogue appears under pressure?
8. What long-term goals require my mental toughness?
9. What excuse do I use that I'm ready to release?
10. How can I expand my tolerance for discomfort?
11. What is one fear I'm capable of facing this year?
12. What commitments matter enough to enforce discipline?
13. How do I regain focus when I feel distracted?
14. What action builds my confidence the fastest?
15. What does mental strength look like daily?
16. What thought patterns sabotage my toughness?
17. How can I replace them with stronger ones?
18. What is one area of life where I want more self-control?
19. What does a resilient version of me do differently?
20. What proof do I have that I am stronger than I think?

SECTION 5 — Turning Challenges Into Opportunities

1. What challenge am I currently facing?
2. What opportunity might be hiding inside it?
3. What perspective shift would change everything?
4. What is this challenge trying to teach me?
5. What new path might be unfolding because of it?
6. How can I approach this challenge strategically, not emotionally?
7. What creative solutions could emerge from this situation?
8. What does "rising with purpose" mean to me?
9. How can I use adversity to strengthen my mission?
10. What new version of myself is being activated?
11. What values does this challenge reinforce?
12. How is this moment shaping my future resilience?
13. What strength will I gain once this challenge is over?
14. How can I transform discomfort into momentum?
15. What support or tools do I need right now?
16. How can this obstacle refine me rather than limit me?
17. What long-term benefit might come from this short-term struggle?
18. Who am I becoming because of what I'm learning?
19. What do I want my future self to thank me for?
20. What breakthrough am I ready to claim after this challenge?

Closing Reflection

Every journal entry you write becomes a conversation with your strongest self. These prompts are not just questions—they are keys. Keys that unlock emotional clarity, mental strength, resilience, self-trust, and a deeper sense of purpose. The more honestly you write, the more powerful this transformation becomes.

Resilience is not built in a single moment—it is built in daily reflections, brave insights, and conscious choices. With every prompt you explore, you step closer to the life you are capable of living. Remember:

You are not journaling to record your life.
You are journaling to rebuild it.

Let these questions guide your evolution. Let your answers guide your rise.

Message from the Author:

I hope you enjoyed this book, I love astrology and knew there was not a book such as this out on the shelf. I love metaphysical items as well. Please check out my other books:

-Life of Government Benefits

-My life of Hell

-My life with Hydrocephalus

-Red Sky

-World Domination:Woman's rule

-World Domination:Woman's Rule 2: The War

-Life and Banishment of Apophis: book 1

-The Kidney Friendly Diet

-The Ultimate Hemp Cookbook

-Creating a Dispensary(legally)

-Cleanliness throughout life: the importance of showering from childhood to adulthood.

-Strong Roots: The Risks of Overcoddling children

-Hemp Horoscopes: Cosmic Insights and Earthly Healing

- Celestial Hemp Navigating the Zodiac: Through the Green Cosmos

-Astrological Hemp: Aligning The Stars with Earth's Ancient Herb

-The Astrological Guide to Hemp: Stars, Signs, and Sacred Leaves

-Green Growth: Innovative Marketing Strategies for your Hemp Products and Dispensary

-Cosmic Cannabis

-Astrological Munchies

-Henry The Hemp

-Zodiacal Roots: The Astrological Soul Of Hemp

- **Green Constellations: Intersection of Hemp and Zodiac**

-Hemp in The Houses: An astrological Adventure Through The Cannabis Galaxy

-Galactic Ganja Guide

Heavenly Hemp
Zodiac Leaves
Doctor Who Astrology
Cannastrology
Stellar Satvias and Cosmic Indicas
Celestial Cannabis: A Zodiac Journey
AstroHerbology: The Sky and The Soil: Volume 1
AstroHerbology:Celestial Cannabis:Volume 2
Cosmic Cannabis Cultivation
The Starry Guide to Herbal Harmony: Volume 1
The Starry Guide to Herbal Harmony: Cannabis Universe: Volume 2
Yugioh Astrology: Astrological Guide to Deck, Duels and more
Nightmare Mansion: Echoes of The Abyss
Nightmare Mansion 2: Legacy of Shadows
Nightmare Mansion 3: Shadows of the Forgotten
Nightmare Mansion 4: Echoes of the Damned
The Life and Banishment of Apophis: Book 2
Nightmare Mansion: Halls of Despair
Healing with Herb: Cannabis and Hydrocephalus
Planetary Pot: Aligning with Astrological Herbs: Volume 1
Fast Track to Freedom: 30 Days to Financial Independence Using AI, Assets, and Agile Hustles
Cosmic Hemp Pathways
How to Become Financially Free in 30 Days: 10,000 Paths to Prosperity
Zodiacal Herbage: Astrological Insights: Volume 1
Nightmare Mansion: Whispers in the Walls
The Daleks Invade Atlantis
Henry the hemp and Hydrocephalus

10X The Kidney Friendly Diet
Cannabis Universe: Adult coloring book

Hemp Astrology: The Healing Power of the Stars

Zodiacal Herbage: Astrological Insights: Cannabis Universe: Volume 2

Planetary Pot: Aligning with Astrological Herbs: Cannabis Universes: Volume 2

Doctor Who: Convergence Protocol – The Replicator War

Nightmare Mansion: Curse of the Blood Moon

The Celestial Stoner: A Guide to the Zodiac

Cosmic Pleasures: Sex Toy Astrology for Every Sign

Hydrocephalus Astrology: Navigating the Stars and Healing Waters

Lapis and the Mischievous Chocolate Bar

Celestial Positions: Sexual Astrology for Every Sign

Apophis's Shadow Work Journal: **:** A Journey of Self-Discovery and Healing

Kinky Cosmos: Sexual Kink Astrology for Every Sign

Digital Cosmos: The Astrological Digimon Compendium

Stellar Seeds: The Cosmic Guide to Growing with Astrology

Apophis's Daily Gratitude Journal

Cat Astrology: Feline Mysteries of the Cosmos

The Cosmic Kama Sutra: An Astrological Guide to Sexual Positions

Unleash Your Potential: A Guided Journal Powered by AI Insights

Whispers of the Enchanted Grove

Cosmic Pleasures: An Astrological Guide to Sexual Kinks

369, 12 Manifestation Journal

Whisper of the nocturne journal(blank journal for writing or drawing)

The Boogey Book

Locked In Reflection: A Chastity Journey Through Locktober

Generating Wealth Quickly:How to Generate $100,000 in 24 Hours

Star Magic: Harness the Power of the Universe

The Flatulence Chronicles: A Fart Journal for Self-Discovery

The Doctor and The Death Moth

Seize the Day: A Personal Seizure Tracking Journal

The Ultimate Boogeyman Safari: A Journey into the Boogie World and Beyond

Whispers of Samhain: 1,000 Spells of Love, Luck, and Lunar Magic: Samhain Spell Book

Apophis's guides:Witch's Spellbook Crafting Guide for Halloween

Frost & Flame: The Enchanted Yule Grimoire of 1000 Winter Spells

The Ultimate Boogey Goo Guide & Spooky Activities for Halloween Fun

Harmony of the Scales: A Libra's Spellcraft for Balance and Beauty

The Enchanted Advent: 36 Days of Christmas Wonders

Nightmare Mansion: The Labyrinth of Screams

Harvest of Enchantment: 1,000 Spells of Gratitude, Love, and Fortune for Thanksgiving

The Boogey Chronicles: A Journal of Nightly Encounters and Shadowy Secrets

The 12 Days of Financial Freedom: A Step-by-Step Christmas Countdown to Transform Your Finances

Sigil of the Eternal Spiral Blank Journal

A Christmas Feast: Timeless Recipes for Every Meal

Holiday Stress-Free Solutions: A Survival Guide to Thriving During the Festive Season

Yu-Gi-Oh! Holiday Gifting Mastery: The Ultimate Guide for Fans and Newcomers Alike

Holiday Harmony: A Hydrocephalus Survival Guide for the Festive Season

Celestial Craft: The Witch's Almanac for 2025 – A Cosmic Guide to Manifestations, Moons, and Mystical Events

Doctor Who: The Toymaker's Winter Wonderland

Tulsa King Unveiled: A Thrilling Guide to Stallone's Mafia Masterpiece

Pendulum Craft: A Complete Guide to Crafting and Using Personalized Divination Tools

Nightmare Mansion: Santa's Eternal Eve

Starlight Noel: A Cosmic Journey through Christmas Mysteries

The Dark Architect: Unlocking the Blueprint of Existence

Surviving the Embrace: The Ultimate Guide to Encounters with The Hugging Molly

The Enchanted Codex: Secrets of the Craft for Witches, Wiccans, and Pagans

Harvest of Gratitude: A Complete Thanksgiving Guide

Yuletide Essentials: A Complete Guide to an Authentic and Magical Christmas

Celestial Smokes: A Cosmic Guide to Cigars and Astrology

Living in Balance: A Comprehensive Survival Guide to Thriving with Diabetes Insipidus

Cosmic Symbiosis: The Venom Zodiac Chronicles

The Cursed Paw of Ambition

Cosmic Symbiosis: The Astrological Venom Journal

Celestial Wonders Unfold: A Stargazer's Guide to the Cosmos (2024-2029)

The Ultimate Black Friday Prepper's Guide: Mastering Shopping Strategies and Savings

Cosmic Sales: The Astrological Guide to Black Friday Shopping

Legends of the Corn Mother and Other Harvest Myths

Whispers of the Harvest: The Corn Mother's Journal

The Evergreen Spellbook

The Doctor Meets the Boogeyman

The White Witch of Rose Hall's SpellBook

The Gingerbread Golem's Shadow: A Study in Sweet Darkness

The Gingerbread Golem Codex: An Academic Exploration of Sweet Myths

The Gingerbread Golem Grimoire: Sweet Magicks and Spells for the Festive Witch

The Curse of the Gingerbread Golem

10-minute Christmas Crafts for kids

Christmas Crisis Solutions: The Ultimate Last-Minute Survival Guide

Gingerbread Golem Recipes: Holiday Treats with a Magical Twist

The Infinite Key: Unlocking Mystical Secrets of the Ages

Enchanted Yule: A Wiccan and Pagan Guide to a Magical and Memorable Season

Dinosaurs of Power: Unlocking Ancient Magick

Astro-Dinos: The Cosmic Guide to Prehistoric Wisdom

Gallifrey's Yule Logs: A Festive Doctor Who Cookbook

The Dino Grimoire: Secrets of Prehistoric Magick

The Gift They Never Knew They Needed

The Gingerbread Golem's Culinary Alchemy: Enchanting Recipes for a Sweetly Dark Feast

A Time Lord Christmas: Holiday Adventures with the Doctor

Krampusproofing Your Home: Defensive Strategies for Yule

Silent Frights: A Collection of Christmas Creepypastas to Chill Your Bones

Santa Raptor's Jolly Carnage: A Dino-Claus Christmas Tale

Prehistoric Palettes: A Dino Wicca Coloring Journey

The Christmas Wishkeeper Chronicles

The Starlight Sleigh: A Holiday Journey

Elf Secrets: The True Magic of the North Pole

Candy Cane Conjurations

Cooking with Kids: Recipes Under 20 Minutes

Doctor Who: The TARDIS Confiscation

The Anxiety First Aid Kit: Quick Tools to Calm Your Mind

Frosty Whispers: A Winter's Tale

The Infinite Key: Unlocking the Secrets to Prosperity, Resilience, and Purpose

The Grasping Void: Why You'll Regret This Purchase

Astrology for Busy Bees: Star Signs Simplified

The Instant Focus Formula: Cut Through the Noise

The Secret Language of Colors: Unlocking the Emotional Codes

Sacred Fossil Chronicles: Blank Journal

The Christmas Cottage Miracle

Feeding Frenzy: Graboid-Inspired Recipes

Manifest in Minutes: The Quick Law of Attraction Guide

The Symbiote Chronicles: Doctor Who's Venomous Journey

Think Tiny, Grow Big: The Minimalist Mindset

The Energy Key: Unlocking Limitless Motivation

New Year, New Magic: Manifesting Your Best Year Yet

Unstoppable You: Mastering Confidence in Minutes

Infinite Energy: The Secret to Never Feeling Drained

Lightning Focus: Mastering the Art of Productivity in a Distracted World

Saturnalia Manifestation Magick: A Guide to Unlocking Abundance During the Solstice

Graboids and Garland: The Ultimate Tremors-Themed Christmas Guide

12 Nights of Holiday Magic

The Power of Pause: 60-Second Mindfulness Practices

The Quick Reset: How to Reclaim Your Life After Burnout

The Shadow Eater: A Tale of Despair and Survival

The Micro-Mastery Method: Transform Your Skills in Just Minutes a Day

Reclaiming Time: How to Live More by Doing Less

Chronovore: The Eternal Nexus

The Mind Reset: Unlocking Your Inner Peace in a Chaotic World
Confidence Code: Building Unshakable Self-Belief
Baby the Vampire Terrier
Baby the Vampire Terrier's Christmas Adventure
Celestial Streams: The Content Creator's Astrology Manual
The Wealth Whisperer: Unlocking Abundance with Everyday Actions
The Energy Equation: Maximize Your Output Without Burning Out
The Happiness Algorithm: Science-Backed Steps to Joyful Living
Stress-Free Success: Achieving Goals Without Anxiety
Mindful Wealth: The New Blueprint for Financial Freedom
The Festive Flavors of New Year: A Culinary Celebration
The Master's Gambit: Keys of Eternal Power
Shadowed Secrets: Groundhog Day Mysteries
Beneath the Burrow: Lessons from the Groundhog
Spring's Whispers: The Groundhog's Prediction
The Limitless Mindset: Unlock Your Untapped Potential
The Focus Funnel: How to Cut Through Chaos and Get Results
Bold Moves: Building Courage to Live on Your Terms
The Daily Shift: Simple Practices for Lasting Transformation
The Quarter-Life Reset: Thriving in Your 20s and 30s
The Art of Shadowplay: Building Your Own Personal Myth
The Eternal Loop: Finding Purpose in Repetition
Burrowing Wisdom: Life Lessons from the Groundhog
Shadow Work: A Groundhog Day Perspective
Love in Bloom: 5-Minute Romantic Gestures
The Shadowspell Codex: Secrets of Forbidden Magick
The Burnout Cure: Finding Balance in a Busy World
The Groundhog Prophecy: Unlocking Seasonal Secrets
Nog Tales: The Spirited History of Eggnog
Six More Weeks: Embracing Seasonal Transitions
The Lumivian Chronicles: Fragments of the Fifth Dimension

Money on Your Mind: A Beginner's Guide to Wealth
The Focus Fix: Breaking Through Distraction
January's Spirit Keepers: Mystical Protectors of the Cold
Creativity Unchained: Unlocking Your Wildest Ideas in 2025
Manifestation Mastery: 365 Days to Rewrite Your Reality
The Groundhog's Mirror: Reflecting on Change
The Weeping Angels' Christmas Curse
Burrowed in Time: A Groundhog Day Journey
Heartbeats: Poems to Share with Your Valentine
Dino Wicca: The Sacred Grimoire of Prehistoric Magick
Courage of the Pride: Finding Your Inner Roar
The Lion's Leap: Bold Moves for Big Results
Healthy Hustle: Achieving Without Overworking
Practical Manifesting: Turning Dreams into Reality in 2025
Jurassic Pharaohs: Unlocking the Magick of Ancient Egypt and Dino Wicca
The Happiness Equation: Small Changes for Big Joy
The Confidence Compass: Finding Your Inner Strength
Whispers in the Hollow: Tales of the Forgotten Beasts
Echoes from the Hollow: The Return of Forgotten Beasts
The Hollow Ascendant: The Rise of the Forgotten Beasts
The Relationship Reset: Building Better Connections
Mastering the Morning: How to Win the Day Before 8 AM
The Shadow's Dance: Groundhog Day Symbolism
Cupid's Kitchen: Quick Valentine's Day Recipes
Valentine's Day on a Budget: Love Without Breaking the Bank
Astrocraft: Aligning the Stars in the World of Minecraft
Forecasting Life: Groundhog Day Reflections
Bleeding Hearts: Twisted Tales of Valentine's Terror
Herbal Smoke Revolution: The Ultimate Guide to Nature's Cigarette Alternative
Winter's Wrath: The Complete Survival Blueprint for Extreme Freezes.

The Groundhog's Shadow: A Tale of Seasons
Burrowed Insights: Wisdom from the Groundhog
Sensual Strings: The Art of Erotic Bondage
Whispered Flames: Unlocking the Power of Fire Play
Forgotten Shadows: A Guide to Cryptids Lost to Time
Six Weeks of Secrets: Groundhog Day's Hidden Messages
Shadows and Cycles: Groundhog Day Reflections
The Art of Love Letters: Crafting the Perfect Message
Romantic Getaways at Home: Turning Your Space into Paradise
Purrfect Brews: A Cat Lover's Guide to Coffee and Companionship
The Groundhog's Wisdom: Timeless Lessons for Modern Life
The Shadow Oracle: Groundhog Day as a Predictor
Emerging from the Burrow: A Journey of Renewal
The Language of Love: Learning Your Partner's Love Style
Authorpreneur: The Ultimate Blueprint for Writing, Publishing, and Thriving as an Author
Weathering the Seasons: Groundhog Day Perspectives
Valentine's Day Magic: A Guide to Romantic Rituals
The Shadow Chronicles: Stories of Groundhog Day
Love and Laughter: Fun Games for Valentine's Day
AstroRealty: Unlocking the Stars for Property Success
The Groundhog's Path: A Guide to Seasonal Balance
Groundhog Day Diaries: Reflections in the Shadow
The Groundhog's Light: Illuminating the Path Ahead
Valentine's Traditions from Around the World
AI Wealth Revolution: Unlocking the Trillionaire Mindset
Love Rekindled: Reigniting Passion in Relationships
Single and Thriving: Self-Love on Valentine's Day
Emerald Legends: Mystical Tales of Ireland
Green Alchemy: Harnessing Nature's Magic
The Hearts of Horror: A Valentine's Day Nightmare

The Leprechaun's Guide to Wealth and Wisdom

Dancing with the Sidhe: Celebrating the Otherworld

Shamrocks and Shadows: Mysteries of the Green Isle

Emerald Energy: Harnessing Luck and Growth

The Gingerbread Golem's Valentine: A Sweetheart's Guide to Love and Enchantment

The Celtic Knot: Weaving Life and Destiny

Green Fire: Elemental Magic for St. Patrick's Day

Clover Chronicles: Finding Your Inner Luck

Ireland's Mystical Creatures: A Field Guide

Gingerbread Golem's Love Almanac

Prowl and Thrive: The Lion's Guide to Success

Love Alchemy: Transforming Your Life Through Heart Energy

WORLD DOMINATION: Woman's Rule 3:The New Life

The Midnight Rose: A Guide to Lunar Love Spells

The Forbidden Letters: Writing Your Own Love Prophecy

Luck and Lore: St. Patrick's Day for Modern Mystics

The Green Path: A Pagan Celebration of Renewal

The Dark Architect's Guide to Reprogramming Reality

Prankster's Paradise: A Guide to Harmless Hijinks

Manifest Your Reality: The Law of Attraction Simplified

The TARDIS Owner's Manual: Understanding the Doctor's Ship: *A complete guide to the TARDIS, its technology, secrets, and mysteries*

Starlit Romance: Astrology Secrets for Finding True Love

The Time Lord's Atlas: A Complete Guide to the Whoniverse: ***A breakdown of the locations, planets, and dimensions explored in Doctor Who***

Sweetheart Shadows: The Dark Side of Love and Attraction

February Fire: Reigniting Passion in Every Area of Life

The Self-Love Toolkit: 5 Ways to Embrace Who You Are

February Sparks: Ignite Your Dreams in 28 Days

March to Success: A 31-Day Action Blueprint
Ancient Paths: The 13 Sacred Principles of Dino Wicca
Echoes of Tomorrow: Navigating the AI Revolution
The Wellness Blueprint: Balancing Mind, Body, and Soul
Green Horizons: Sustainable Living for a Better Tomorrow
The AI Wealth Code: How to Make Millions with Automation
AI-Powered Creativity: Writing, Art, and Music for Profit
Extinction Rites: Rebirthing Your Soul Through Prehistoric Magick
Sacred Serpents tarot
Celestial Enchantment blank journal
Star Strains
Culinary Journeys: Exploring Global Flavors at Home
The Hollowvale Curse
The Hollowvale Harvest
The Egg of Transformation: Awakening Your Inner Power
Blooming Into Power: A Wiccan Guide to Spring Awakening
The Nightmare Nexus: The Third Doctor's Perilous Haunting
Digital Detox: Reclaiming Your Life in a Connected World
Ostara's Path: Walking the Spiral of Renewal
The Sacred Hare
Financial Freedom: Building Wealth in the Modern Age
Spring's Cauldron: Stirring the Waters of Change
The Hollowvale Pact
Quantum Consciousness: The Science of Reality Shifting
The Hollowvale Hunger
The Sacred Waters Within: A Witch's Guide to Hydrocephalus Magick
The Raven's Nest: Building a Life of Unshakable Stability
AI and the Human Mind: The Future of Intelligence
The Hollowvale Reckoning
Timeless Love: Building and Maintaining Lasting Relationships

The Raven's Roar: Unlocking Unstoppable Confidence
Raven Sight: Awakening Intuition and Inner Wisdom
The Butterfly Effect: Small Changes, Big Transformations
Taming the Boogeyman: How to Conquer Your Inner Fears
The Magick of Green: Awakening Earth's Energy in You
The Entrepreneurial Mindset: Secrets to Business Success
The Hollowvale End
The Shadow Luck Ritual: Reclaiming Power from Your Dark Side
Spring Magick for Beginners: A Simple Guide to Seasonal Energy Work
Doctor Who: The Hollowvale Conundrum
The March of Miracles: Unlocking Synchronicities in Spring
Unveiling the Cosmos: A Guide to Stargazing and Space Exploration
The Ultimate Guide to Surviving an Economic Collapse
The AI Gold Rush: How to Profit from the AI Revolution
Bastet's Shadow: The Hidden Power of Feline Magick
The Bastet Codex: Unlocking the Goddess's Magickal Secrets
Purring Spells: Harnessing Bastet's Healing Frequencies
Bastet's Nine Lives: Rebirth, Transformation, and Immortality Spells
Primal Currents: Hydrocephalus Magick in the Path of Dino Wicca
The Digital Gold Rush: Mastering E-Commerce and Online Sales
Future Shock: Adapting to the Next Decade of Change
The Quantum Mindset: Think Like a Billionaire
Sacred Motherhood: Awakening the Divine Feminine Within
The Mother's Spellbook: Enchantments for Love, Protection, and Prosperity
The Witch's Guide to Parenting: Raising Empowered and Intuitive Children

The Magick of Motherhood: Reclaiming Your Power Through Rituals

The Pagan Path to Self-Love: A Goddess's Guide to Worth and Confidence

Wild Woman Magick: Unleashing Your Primal Power

The Money Magnet Blueprint: Unlocking Unlimited Wealth

Biohacking 101: Unlock Your Body's Full Potential

The Wild Father: A Pagan Guide to Strength and Wisdom

The Sacred Masculine: Unlocking Your Inner Power

The Druid's Compass

The Warrior's Mindset

The Father's Fire

Odin's Path

Ancestral Bonds

The House That Whispers

The Magician's Code

The Wild Hunt

The Green Man's Path

The Altar of Success

The Shadow and the Sword

The High Priestess's Guide to Energy Healing

The Lunar Mother

The Sacred Self-Care Grimoire

The Womb Wisdom Codex

The Wheel of the Mother

The Witch's Guide to Manifestation

The Q2 Reset

The Ultimate Guide to AI-Powered Passive Income

Escape the 9-5

AI Feline Fortunes

The Tear-Stained Grimoire

Razorblade Runes

Cemetery Sirens

The Midnight Wristwatch
The Town That Forgets
AI Horror & Creepypasta
The Hollow Frequency
The Breach Echo
The Quiet Between Worlds
The Sigil of Tharan-Khul
Summon the Vault of Y'ha'ten
The Becoming Codex
The Profit of Az'ra-nar
The Drowned Logos
Echoes of the Eldritch Will
The Deep Ledger
Necronomicon of Networth
Covenant of the Wealthwyrm
The Whisperer's Manifesto
The Rites of Azh-K'luth
The Ark of the Crawling Coin
The Tithe of Shadows
Inkheart Abyss
The Timewinds of Y'ha-nthlei
The Spiral Labyrinth of Azag-Nirrh
The Gallifreyan Heresy of the Black Pharaoh
The Psalms of Nyog-Sotha
Black Rain Alchemy
The Infinite Maw
The Entropic Blueprint
The Oracle of Sh'guul
The Book of Breach
The Drowned Saint's Testament
Dreamcraft of the Sleeper God
The Silence Market
Cthonomics: The Dark Wealth Algorithm

Invocation of the Ten-Eyed King
Wealthbound to the Wyrm Below
Become the Unnameable
Codex of the Sovereign Flame
Rituals of Relentless Becoming
The Shadow Ascends
The Eyes Beneath You
The Will That Wakes Worlds
Silence Is a Weapon
The Mirror That Screams
The Whisper Between Moments
The Mind That Devours Fear
The Myth of the Finished Self
The Architect of Your Madness
The Voice You've Buried
The Discipline of Madness
Stormborn: Awakening Your Inner Tempest
The Mind That Ate Time
Unbind Your Becoming
The Pact You Owe Yourself
The Devourer's Diet
The Acid That Carves the Path
The Tower You Must Burn
The Breath Between Worlds
Speak Like the Deep
The Labyrinth Within
The Spine of the Sea God
Rejection Is a Portal
The Crown You Refused
The Scar Is the Spell
The Lightless Flame
The Habit of Becoming Horrific
ChickenJockey Chaos

The Gatekeeper Within
You Are Not Your Name
The Compass of the Mad
The Archive of Unsent Letters
What the Mirror Can't Show You
The Knife You Needed
Worship Nothing, Become Everything
The Other Voice
The Body the World Forgot
The Vein of the Void
The Black Bone Codex
The Puzzle of the Hidden Self (Millennium Puzzle)
The Eye That Sees the Lie *(Millennium Eye)*
The Ring of Return (Millennium Ring)
The Rod of Relentless Will ***(Millennium Rod)***
The Tally of the Soul (Millennium Tauk/Necklace)
The Key to the Locked Timeline (Millennium Key)
The Scale of Sacred Decisions (Millennium Scales)
Inferno Bites: The UnOfficial Minecraft Lava Cookbook
Rot in the Attic
Prana: The Hidden Force of Your Infinite Self
The Shadow Realm Within: Transforming Darkness Into Destiny
The Borderland Collapse
Claws of Protection: Bastet's Defensive Magick
Mr. Ring-a-Ding's Madness
Yugioh Astrology: Celestial Deckcraft and Duel Destiny (2026–2027 Edition)
The Seal You Signed: Unlocking the Power You Once Feared
The Puzzle of Infinite Minds: Unlocking the Mentalism Hidden Within
The Eye That Mirrors the All: Secrets of Inner Reflection
Doctor Who: The Toymaker's Broadcast

The Rod of Eternal Flow: Commanding the Currents of Vibration

Golden Eyes of Bastet: Enhancing Psychic Vision

The Key of Dual Forces: Balance Within the Polarity

The Scales of Living Rhythm: Timing the Dance of Life

The Necklace of Hidden Cause: Weaving the Webs of Fate

The Ring of Secret Masters: Rising Through the All Within All

Daggers of the Dying Deep

Bastet's Wealth and Fortune Magick: Prosperity Rituals of the Goddess

The Tide that Speaks

The Scrolls of Petosiris: 13 Rituals from the Feathered Eye

Petosiris and the Living Plague of Osirion

Feline Fire: Bastet's Passion and Love Magick

The Star Altar of Petosiris

Bastet's Whiskers: Supernatural Sensory Magick

The Bastet Grimoire

Feeding the Shadows

The Mouthless Prayer

The Spiral Wound

Becoming the Ibis: Lessons from Petosiris's Mind

The Crimson Coven: Cola Magick for Sweet Dominion

Sacred Cat's Paw

The Soda Zodiac: A Flavor for Every Sign

Covenant of the Crawling Flame

The Ink of Ish'Zur

Frothroot: The Thirst That Ate the World

The Golden Glyphs of Prosperity

The Etherbind Codex

Echoes of the Resistance: Reclaiming the You That Survived

Harnessed Minds: Breaking Free from Mental Control

The Eyes in the Smoke

Rootwake: The Carbon Covenant
Skitter Logic: Unlearning the Fear That Built You
Doctor Who: The World That Froths
Rootwake: The Fizz That Rewrites Flesh
Rootwake: Frothfather of the World
The Holly Pact: Blood Beneath the Mistletoe
The 2nd Mass Principle: Building Unbreakable Tribes
Web of Wits: A Survival Guide to Encounters with Anasi the Spider (Aunt Nancy)
The Hexbreaking Handbook: Effective Spells to Remove Curses
Pop Alchemy: Transform Your Life One Sip at a Time
The Mason Code: Leading in Unleadable Times
Petosiris and the Fifth Chamber of Thoth
The Ether Seed Within
The Parent of Tomorrow
Petosiris's Pyramid of Perpetual Wealth
Unlearn the World
Grimoire of the Hollow Tongue
Zodiac Weeds: Finding Your Strain Through the Stars
Aquarius Rises in the Bank
The Sugar God's Smile
The Skinclock Reversal: Biohacking the Face of Time
Debtburn: How to Obliterate What You Owe Forever
The Ice Cream Oracle: What Your Cone Says About Your Future
Silence Is Sovereignty: The Power of Being Unreadable
The Wind That Whispers Through Stone
Path of the Four Directions
Doctor Who: The Maestro's Symphony of Endings
Oxygen Grail: Breathing to Undo the Clock
Zodiacal Collapse: When Stars Devour Time
Teachings from the Red Sand Silence

Doctor Who: Omega – The Broken Equation
Memory Wipe Your Past: Start Over Like a MiB
Mitochondria Prime: Ignite the Core of Youth
A Nest of Roaches
Grub from the Galaxy: MiB Recipes You'll Never Forget
Whiskers of Power: Bastet's Guide to Inner Sovereignty
The Gift Must Cost Them: Negotiation Through Unequal Exchange
The Worm Guys' Wealth Code: Hustle Like an Alien
Bug Out: The Edgar Method for Ruthless Goal Setting
Weaving Life with Spiderwoman's Pattern
Doctor Who: The Rani's Renaissance
How to Get a Job (If You're a Puppygirl)
Speak Through Others: The Art of Proxy Power
T-Rex Your Trauma: Reclaim the Power of Your Primal Self
The Black Briefcase: How MiB Stay Wealthy in Silence
The Thirst Beyond Reason: Understanding Diabetes Insipidus From the Inside Out
Backwoods Witchcraft for Billionaires: The Pagan Path from Dirt Roads to Gold Roads
The Moonshine Grimoire: Fermented Spells for Abundance
The Nameless Geometry
The Wraith's Mixtape: Spellcasting with Songs of Sorrow
The Gallifreyan Gentleman: Silent Wealth, Sonic Confidence, and the Doctor's Code of Living
Sugar Water Confidence
Dino Totems: Spirit Guides from Earth's First Gods
Pumpkin Sigils & Ritual Smoke
The Hózhó Compass
The Distortus Discipline – Order from Inner Mutation
Witchcraft for the Cold-Blooded Soul
Moonlight Over the Blessingway
Water, Interrupted: When the Body Forgets How to Hold On

Deformed but Divine: Embracing Your Asymmetry
Hexes in the Henhouse: The Farm Witch's Guide to Power
The Reversed Flame: A Grimoire of Inverted Power
Salt, Cells, and Sanity: Reclaiming Balance with Diabetes Insipidus
King of the Broken: Crowning the Flawed Self
Moonlight Scars: Emo Moon Magick and the Art of Lunar Sorrow
Noose Spells: Magick of the Hanging Rope
The Goth Cathedral: Rituals of the Broken and Beautiful
The Cretaceous Codex: Dino Spirits and Fossil Magick
The Turkey Bones Ritual
Nine Lives of Manifestation: Unlocking Bastet's Reality Codes
Chaos Muscles: Building Strength from Twisted Pain
Emo Blood Magick: The Veins of Power
The 3AM Flood: Nighttime Urination, Sleep Loss, and the DI Spiral
The Silence Between the Stars
The Lemon Method: Sour Your Way to Success
Starlit Sovereign
The Rite of Twelve Gates: Walking the Gates of the Duat.
Cornbread and Conjure: Recipes for Riches and Rootwork
The Black Rose Rituals: Emo Love Spells and Obsession Magick
The Eternal Goodbye: Death Magick and Rebirth Rituals
Sinkrot: The Drain That Remembers
The Hybrid Mindset: Thinking Beyond Evolution
Bone Dry: Navigating Dehydration Before It Breaks You
Wreathcraft: Winter Sigils and Yuletide Spells
The Rite of Twelve Mouths
S'mores of the Damned: Haunted Recipes for Halloween Night

Rethink the Drink: A Beverage Survival Guide for DI Warriors

The Shadow Chord: Guitar Magick and Sonic

Malformed Yet Majestic: Leading When You Feel Wrong Inside

The Cursed Diary: Ink-Stained Spells of the Emo Soul

Anxiety Off Switch: Emergency Reset for a Fried Nervous System

The Energy Heist: How to Take Back Your Life from Drainers

Beyond the Bathroom: Rebuilding Your Social Life With DI

Coyote's Gift for Decision Makers

Ghoul-Goo: Spooky S'mores You'll Die For

Echoes in the Mirror: Scrying and Self-Destruction Magick

Thread and Thorn: Stitching Spells from Rural Cloth

The Mogwai Mind: Building Untouchable Wealth from Small Ideas

Be Your Own Guide: Trust Your Inner Compass

Hormones in Chaos: The Endocrine Puzzle of Diabetes Insipidus

ChronoCleanse: Detox Your Biological Timeline

The Limb You Hide Is the One That Saves You

Leaves, Bones, and Whisper Spells

The Dinosaur Mindset: Prehistoric Tactics for Modern Wealth

Clawing Back Control: A Bastet Method for Boundaries and Empowerment

Samhain Codes of the Forgotten

Orange Alchemy: The Autumnal Spellbook

Monster Within, Master Without

The Sigil That Sleeps

Hearthcraft: Yule Hearth Sigils and Winter Warmth Spells

Temple of the Purring Moon: Rituals from Bastet's Lineage

When the Earth Remembers Your Footsteps

Food for Mood: Eat to Heal Depression, Not Just Survive It
Witch of the Kudzu Vine: Southern Pagan Wealth Secrets
The Invisible Diagnosis: Advocating for Yourself With DI
The Coffin's Lullaby: Sleep Magick and Nightmares as Portals
Ashes of the Will: Rituals for Erasing the Self
The Fracture Rite: Shattering the Magickal Core
Funeral Candles: The Art of Emo Flame Magick
The Black Grimoire: A Blank Ritual for Writing in Absence
Phantom Thirst: A Halloween Survival Guide for Diabetes Insipidus
The Hollow Crown: Emo Royalty and Magick of the Outcast King
Sandpainting for the Soul
Falling Into Balance: Using the Extra Hour to Recalibrate Life
100 Southern Superstitions That Still Work
The DI Child: A Parent's Guide to Raising Hydrated, Happy Kids
The Jungle of Shame: Escaping the Hidden Lab of Doubt
The Witch's Toast: S'mores Spells and Creepy Confections
The Hoodoo Pantry: Spells from the Mason Jar
The Immortal Fortune: Secret Wealth Lessons from Captain Jack Harkness
The Specter's Embrace: Magick for Channeling Ghostly Lovers
Grateful Waters: A Thanksgiving Survival Guide for Diabetes Insipidus
The Seizure Gospel
Harvestbind: Autumn Sigils and Samhain Spells
Doctor Who: The Algorithmic Awakening
Silent Nights, Steady Waters: A Christmas Survival Guide for Diabetes Insipidus
The Extra Hour Effect: How One Hour Can Transform Everything

Blade Between the Breaths
Running with the Mountain Shadows
Echoes of the Failed Experiment – Becoming a Living Legacy
Swamp Witches & River Ghosts: Real Southern Hauntings
Cornbread Prophecies: Magical Recipes from a Southern Table
Doctor Who: The Signal in the Star
Bloomcraft: Spring Sigils and Equinox Enchantments
Vanisher: How to Disappear from the Internet Without Losing Your Life
The Ultimate Christmas Cookie Cookbook
The Unbreakable Parent: How to Mentally Survive Raising Kids in a Broken World
Time Debt: How to Reclaim the Hours You Didn't Know You Lost
One Month, One Million: Unconventional Cash Creation Tactics
Doctor Who: The Cyber Conversion Protocol
Black Friday Frenzy: The Art of Finding Hidden Online Deals
The Grimoire Buried Under the Apple Tree
Digital Couponing Masterclass: Your Step-by-Step Guide to Black Friday Savings
The Fire Inside the Flint
Shadows on the Ceiling: The Emo Guide to Astral Magick
The Bone-Eaters Beneath Us
Black Friday Bundle Blueprint: Creating Irresistible Product Packages for Maximum Sales
Thirteen Nights of Unbinding
Doctor Who: Engines of Influence
Pumpkin Spice Alchemy: Recipes of Fire and Frost
When Raptor Met Rexy: Prehistoric Lessons in Wild Romance
Oblivion's Candle: Burn the Path Behind You

Campfire Curses and Chocolate: A Halloween S'mores Grimoire

The Wallet That Wasn't Mine: Breaking Free from Inherited Scarcity

The Cola Zodiac: What Your Fizz Says About Your Fate

Frostfire Fortune: Unlocking Winter's Hidden Prosperity

Signal Jamming: Detox Your Brain from Info Overload

The Dust of the Forgotten Rite

The Golden Cat Sigils: Drawing Power in Bastet's Name

Mud Magick: The Prosperity of Getting Dirty

Savory Spicefall: Beyond the Pumpkin Pie

Pumpkin Spice Apothecary Kitchen

The Pumpkin Spice Economy: Turning Trends into Billions

The Ember Veil: 13 Nights of Fire Magick

Financial Freeze: When Earning Triggers Panic

The Gingerbread Alchemist: Sweet Recipes with a Twist

Biosynth Power: Programming Yourself from Scratch

Echoes from the Talking Circle

Truffle Alchemy: Fungus of Fortune

Spores of Power: The Truffle Witch's Handbook

Doctor Who: The Tower That Speaks

The Mycelium Veil: Truffle Magick Unbound

Broke But Ashamed: Healing the Shame Wound of Debt

The Evergreen Mind: Growth Through Winter Stillness

The Black Veil Truffle Rite

The Voice Beneath Symbols

Witchlight on the Bayou: Swamp Spells for Sovereignty

I Grew Up Poor and Now I Sabotage My Success

The Lantern of Hollow Souls

Shutdown Survival: A Citizen's Guide to Thriving When Government Stops

When Abundance Feels Like a Threat: Healing the Hidden Fears of Enough

The Scarecrow Grimoire
Owls of the October Veil
Candlewax and Curses: A Halloween Spellbook
Excavating the Inner Fossil – Transforming Fossilized Thoughtforms into Tools of Power
The Yule Witch's Spellbook: Magick for the Holiday Season
Haunted Christmas: Ghost Stories for Winter Nights
The Christmas Survival Guide: Thriving Through the Chaos
The Bone Orchard Rites
Haunted Commerce: The Ghost in the Marketplace
When Money Triggers the Inner Child
Silent Night with the Silence: A Christmas Thriller
The Lightning Crown: Living and Leading Through Seizures
TARDIS Tidings: Festive Stories from the Whoniverse
Autumn Reset: Slowing Down Without Falling Behind
The Trillion Dollar Soul: Rewriting the Currency of Reality
Truffle Eclipse Magick
Micro-Manifestations: Quick Magick That Works
5-Minute Rituals for Busy Witches
The Marshmallow Massacre: Halloween Treats with a Sinister Twist
Blood and Blackberry Thorns
Magickal Mornings: Rituals for a Blessed Christmas Day
Embers of the All-Hallows Fire
The Pumpkin Market Collapse
The Hour You Gained: Transforming Time Into Power
The Chamber Must Be Sealed: Mastering the Power of Controlled Access
The Cursed Manuscript of Petosiris
The Festive Hearth: Creating Holiday Traditions
Darkness Rising: Thriving as Nights Grow Longer
Harvesting Time: Turning the Year's End Into Your New Beginning

Petosiris and the 13th Zodiac Key
Wagewound: When Paychecks Become Identity Prisons
Walls That Watch
The Silent Feast: Rituals of Power in the Longest Night
The Distortus Legacy : Becoming a Deformed King in a Perfect World
The Hollow Masks
The Gratitude Furnace: Forging Gold from Thanks
Feast of Inner Gold: Eating for Energy and Enlightenment
Haunted Commerce: The Season of Spending Spirits
Fear Bonds: How Panic Creates Profit
Black Friday E-Commerce Playbook: Sales Tactics to Skyrocket Your Holiday Revenue
Budgeting for Black Friday: A Holiday Savings Planner
Haunting the Harvest Moon
The Warrior's Water: Emergency Preparedness for People With DI
The First Sip of the Year: A New Year's Survival Guide for Diabetes Insipidus
Doctor Who: The Thirteenth Node
The Unseen Struggle: Mental Health, Anxiety, and Chronic Thirst
The Hearth's Hidden Ledger: Counting Energies as Currency
The Gift Alchemist: Turning Any Offering Into Gold
The Papyrus of the Bound Spirit
The Magick of Leftovers: Transmutation in the Fridge
Frost and Fortune: Christmas Wealthcraft for the Modern Magus
Last-Minute Gifts: Creative Ideas on a Budget
10 Secrets to Surviving Holiday Crowds
The Witch's Dow Jones
The Witches' Graveyard Shift
Pumpkin Sigils: Carving Rites for Midnight Power

The Secret Shopper's Black Friday Guide: How to Get Early Access and VIP Deals
Fever in the Foundation
The Neuralyzer Reset: Reprogram Your Morning Routine
Lightning Lessons of the White Painted Woman
The Enchanted Snowflake
The Magic Sip: Surviving Disney Parks with Diabetes Insipidus
The One Who Draws Through You
Santa's Secrets: A Magical Holiday Planner
Silent Bells, Loud Miracles: Self-Help for the Season of Stillness
The Sugar Spell Codex: Confectionary Magick of Christmas
Autumn Hexcraft: Fallen Leaves, Fallen Barriers
Sleep Like a Fortress: Build a Life Where Insomnia Can't Survive
Nowhere Was Ever Home
Christmas Under the Stars: A Celestial Holiday Guide
Rentproof: How to Never Be Evicted Again
Workless: Escape the 9-5 Without Being Broke
The Gilded Gift: A Wealth Altar for Christmas Morning
The Black Friday Grimoire
The Hollowing: Ceremonies of Spiritual Collapse
Doctor Who: The Nameless Signal
Where the Eagle Hides His Courage
The Dwarf Tyrant's Ascent: Claiming Power in a World of Giants
The Currency of the Dead: Trading with Spectral Bankers
The Icebound Witch: Survival and Magick in the Cold
The Emergency Money Mind: Constant Crisis, Zero Calm
Thirst & Roses: A Valentine's Survival Guide for Diabetes Insipidus

Springing Into Clarity: Mastering the Energy Shift of Daylight Saving

Speed of the Nanotyrant: Agile Strategies for Life's Hunt

The 90-Day Reset: A Science-Backed Guide to Reinvent Yourself Before the New Year

The Coil of Thorns

Timegates Unleashed

Dopamine Fasting 2.0: Rewiring Your Brain in a World of Overstimulation

The Nanotyrannus Mutation: Embracing Your Differentiated Form

Unwritten January: How to Use the Blank Page of the Year to Re-Author Your Life

Feast of the Forgotten Spirits: Ancestor Magick for the Holidays

The Burnout Codex: A System for Thriving Beyond Stress

I Don't Deserve to Have Money

When the King Doesn't See You: The Shadow Predator's Guide

The Reset Ritual :A Guide to Shedding Last Year's Weight—Emotional and Physical—by Spring Cleaning Your Soul

Calendar Alchemy: Learn to Bend Time and Productivity around Your Natural Rhythms

The Mirror Contract: A One-Sentence Agreement with Yourself that Unlocks Real Change

The Nile Formula: Sacred Flow for Millionaire Minds

Forward Momentum: Productivity Rituals for the Lost Hour

Harvest Gold: Wealth Magick of Pumpkin Spice Commerce

The Magick of Christmas Lights: Illuminating Holiday Rituals

Cranberry Crown: Royal Self-Worth through Ritual Meals

Petosiris and the Worms of the Feathered Throne

The Evergreen Equation: Self-Help for Sustained Growth

The Rain Will Wash Us Away: Emo Weather Magick
Snowlight Shadows: Magick Under Frozen Stars
Doctor Who: Merger of Empires
The Light Within the Feast: Magickal Wealth of Yuletide Flame
Momentum Machines: Small Habits Designed to Snowball into Unstoppable Forward Motion
Calm Spells: Magickal Solutions for Anxiety Relief
Santa's Final List: The Naughty Never Leave
The Mystic's Guide to Banishing Worry
The Silence Dividend: Turning Quiet Mornings into Compounding Growth All Year
Charmed Stillness: Rituals to Ease the Mind
Blood Spiral Ascension
The Vanishing Heart Invocation
Crystal Calm: Harnessing Stones for Anxiety
The Nano Tyrant Code: Strength in the Small Predator
The Energy Ledger: Accounting Methods for Vitality, Not Just Money
Snowglobe Mindset: Shake Up Your Thoughts, Settle Into Peace
The Weight of the Feather: Anubis's Codes for Soul Balance
Pocket Peppermint Power: Tiny Rituals for Big Holiday Energy
Shadowkeeper of the Golden Jackal: Anubis's Path to Energetic Protection
The Witch's Breath: Anxiety Relief Through Magickal Breathing
The Tiny Ember: Pocket Motivation for Cold Days
Stocking Sorcery: Mini Spells for Holiday Luck and Prosperity
Warm Hands, Steady Heart: Micro Grounding for Winter Anxiety

The Jackal's Lantern: Guide-Lights for Walking the Dark Path

Anubis's Silent Steps: Rituals for Stealth, Peace & Emotional Quiet

The Bonewake Protocol

Extinction-Proof: How to Outlive Trends, Trauma, and Time

The Fourth Doctor: The Eccentric Wanderer

The Second Doctor: Chaos and Charm in the TARDIS (Patrick Troughton, 1966–1969)

The Third Doctor: Earthbound Defender of Time (Jon Pertwee, 1970–1974)

The First Doctor: Genesis of the Time Lord (William Hartnell, 1963–1966)

The Fourth Doctor: The Eccentric Wanderer *(Tom Baker, 1974–1981)*

The Fifth Doctor: Elegance and Empathy (Peter Davison, 1982–1984)

The Sixth Doctor: A Kaleidoscope of Conflict (Colin Baker, 1984–1986)

The Seventh Doctor: The Strategist of Shadows (Sylvester McCoy, 1987–1989)

The Eighth Doctor: A Time Lord's Renaissance (Paul McGann, 1996)

The War Doctor: A Time Lord's Burden (John Hurt, 2013)

The Ninth Doctor: The Healer of Worlds
(Christopher Eccleston, 2005)

The Tenth Doctor: The Lonely Hero (David Tennant, 2005–2010)

The Eleventh Doctor: The Madman in a Box (Matt Smith, 2010–2013)

The Twelfth Doctor: The Rebel with a Cause (Peter Capaldi, 2013–2017)

The Thirteenth Doctor: Breaking the Mold
(Jodie Whittaker, 2017–2022)

The Fourteenth Doctor: A New Beginning (David Tennant, 2022–2023)

The Fifteenth Doctor: Rewriting the Stars
(Ncuti Gatwa, 2023–2025)

Santa's Shortcut to Success: Micro Habits for a Better New Year

The Midnight Cocoa Manifesto: Comfort Rituals for Hard Nights

Why I Can't Save: Trauma Blocks to Financial Planning

Dino Brain, Mega Goals: Rewire Yourself for Savage Success.

Jurassic Profit: Unearth Your Inner Millionaire Fossil

Scales & Softness: Dating with Dino Heart

Carnotaurus Dreams.

Red Willow Thinking.

Reindeer Resilience: How to Keep Going When You're Exhausted

Candlewick Courage: Lighting Strength in Dark Seasons.

Elf-Mode Focus: Fast Attention Fixes for Busy Seasons

Futureproof Feelings: Emotional Skill-Building for Resilience No Matter What the New Year Brings

The 90-Day Rewire: Transform Your Neural Pathways Before Spring Blooms

Jolly Rich: Christmas Micro-Money Magick for Fast Prosperity.

Gingerbread Gratitude: Mini Practices for a Happier Holiday

Trauma-Spending: When Money Becomes a Drug

Goal Skeletons: Build Minimalist Frameworks for Resolutions That Last

The Snarl Strategy: Growling Back at a World That Silenced You

The Hourglass Reset: Reclaiming What the Clock Took

Yule Claw: Dino Rites of Light in the Darkness

Sacred Circles: Grounding Rituals for Anxious Souls

Clockstopper's Gut: Rebuilding the Core of Time

Winterfire Drive: Harness the Cold Season's Stillness to Ignite Deep Motivation

The 5-Minute Productivity Hack: Small Steps to Big Results

Light Ascending: A Self-Help Guide to Longer Days

Inner Economy: Trade Self-Doubt for Confidence Like a High-Value Currency

Simple Success: Decluttering Your Life for Better Results

Get Some Tarot cards: https://www.makeplayingcards.com/sell/apophis-occult-shop

Get some shirts: https://www.bonfire.com/store/apophis-shirt-emporium/

Instagrams:
@apophis_enterprises,
@apophisbookemporium,
@apophisscardshop
Twitter: @apophisenterpr1
Tiktok:@apophisenterprise
Youtube: @sg1fan23477
Hive: @sg1fan23477
CheeLee: @SG1fan23477

Podcast: Apophis Chat Zone: https://open.spotify.com/show/5zXbrCLEV2xzCp8ybrfHsk?si=fb4d4fdbdce44dec

Newsletter: https://apophiss-newsletter-27c897.beehiiv.com/

If you want to support me or see posts of other projects that I have come over to: **buymeacoffee.com/mpetchinskg**

I post there daily several times a day

Get your Dinowicca or Christmas themed digital products, especially Santa Raptor songs and other musics. Here: **https://sg1fan23477.gumroad.com**

Apophis Yuletide Digital has not only digital Christmas items, but it will have all things with Dinowicca as well as other Digital products.

www.ingramcontent.com/pod-product-compliance
Lightning Source LLC
LaVergne TN
LVHW020235210926
848481LV00016B/2336